Big Buses

Lynn Peppas

Crabtree Publishing Company

www.crabtreebooks.com

Created by Bobbie Kalman

Author
Lynn Peppas

Editorial director
Kathy Middleton

Project editor
Paul Challen

Editors
Adrianna Morganelli
Reagan Miller

Proofreaders
Janine Belzak
Rachel Stuckey

Photo research
Melissa McClellan

Design
Melissa McClellan
Tibor Choleva

Print coordinator
Katherine Berti

Production coordinator
Margaret Amy Salter

Prepress technicians
Margaret Amy Salter
Ken Wright

Consultant
Stuart Harding, Gray Coach

Illustrations
All illustrations by Leif Peng

Photographs
Bigstock.com: © Andrey Pavlov (title page); © Gautier Willaume (page 4 bottom); © Vicki France (page 9 top, page 12); © Valeriy Ivanov (page 13 top); © Chris Green (page 15 top); © Olga van de Veer (pages 14–15); © Annie Suh (page 21 top); © Stephen Spreadbury(page 27 top inset)
Dreamstime.com: © Zhang Liwei (page 5 bottom); © Nicholas Burningham (pages 6–7); © Daniel Raustadt (page 8); © Zmaj011 (page 9 bottom); © Jmarijs (page 11 bottom); © View77 (page 14 top); © Popa Bogdan (page 16 bottom); © Steve Dunn (page 20); © Somatuscani (page 21 bottom); © Thomas Perkins (page 23 top); © Luis Eduardo Varela Solari (page 24); © Szymon Borowski (page 25 top); © Mlan61 (page 25 bottom); © Andrew Chambers (page 31)
istockphoto: © Christopher Futcher (table of contents page); © Digital Planet Design (page 23 bottom)
© Melissa McCllellan (page 10)
Public Domain: © Secondarywaltz (page 13 bottom); © Arriva436 (page 28)
Shutterstock.com: cover; © Nataliya Hora (page 4 top); © Faraways (page 5 top); © Glenda M. Powers (page 11 top); © Inga Nielsen (page 16 top); © Ryan Hurry (page 17); © stocksnapp (page 18); © Leenvdb (page 14 bottom); © Christophe Testi (page 19 top, page 30); © Carsten Reisinger (page 22); © Andrey Pavlov (pages 26–27); © Chris Jenner (page 29 top and bottom)

Library and Archives Canada Cataloguing in Publication

Peppas, Lynn
   Big buses / Lynn Peppas.

(Vehicles on the move)
Includes index.
Issued also in electronic format.
ISBN 978-0-7787-2726-2 (bound).--ISBN 978-0-7787-2733-0 (pbk.)

   1. Buses--Juvenile literature. I. Title. II. Series: Vehicles on the move

TL232.P46 2011   j629.222'33   C2011-900136-5

Library of Congress Cataloging-in-Publication Data

Peppas, Lynn.
   Big buses / Lynn Peppas.
     p. cm. -- (Vehicles on the move)
   Includes index.
   ISBN 978-0-7787-2733-0 (pbk. : alk. paper) -- ISBN 978-0-7787-2726-2 (reinforced library binding : alk. paper) -- ISBN 978-1-4271-9695-8 (electronic (pdf))
   1. Buses--Juvenile literature. 2. Subways--Juvenile literature. I. Title.
TL232.P37 2011
629.222'33--dc22

2010052345

Crabtree Publishing Company

www.crabtreebooks.com   1-800-387-7650

Printed in the U.S.A./022011/CJ20101228

Published in Canada
Crabtree Publishing
616 Welland Ave.
St. Catharines, ON
L2M 5V6

Published in the United States
Crabtree Publishing
PMB 59051
350 Fifth Avenue, 59th Floor
New York, New York 10118

Published in the United Kingdom
Crabtree Publishing
Maritime House
Basin Road North, Hove
BN41 1WR

Published in Australia
Crabtree Publishing
386 Mt. Alexander Rd.
Ascot Vale (Melbourne)
VIC 3032

Contents

Going places on a bus

Buses are vehicles that move many people. Vehicles are machines that move from one place to another. They come in different colors, shapes, and sizes. The world's largest bus can carry up to 300 people.

Bus passengers can relax while getting where they need to go.

People ride buses in countries all over the world.

Sharing the ride

It is cleaner for the Earth when many people share one ride. Most vehicles, even buses, burn **fossil fuels** for power. Vehicles that burn fossil fuels pollute the air. But if the people who take buses drove cars instead of sharing a bus they would make a lot more pollution.

Bus-only lanes can make traveling by bus faster than driving.

*Buses are better for the **environment** than cars. One busload of people can remove more than 40 cars from the highway.*

Good to go

Buses are big, heavy vehicles. Some weigh more than 16 tons (15,000 kilograms). Engines give them power to move. Buses have six or more rubber wheels. The number of wheels depends on the size of the bus. Buses have windows all around so passengers can look outside as they travel.

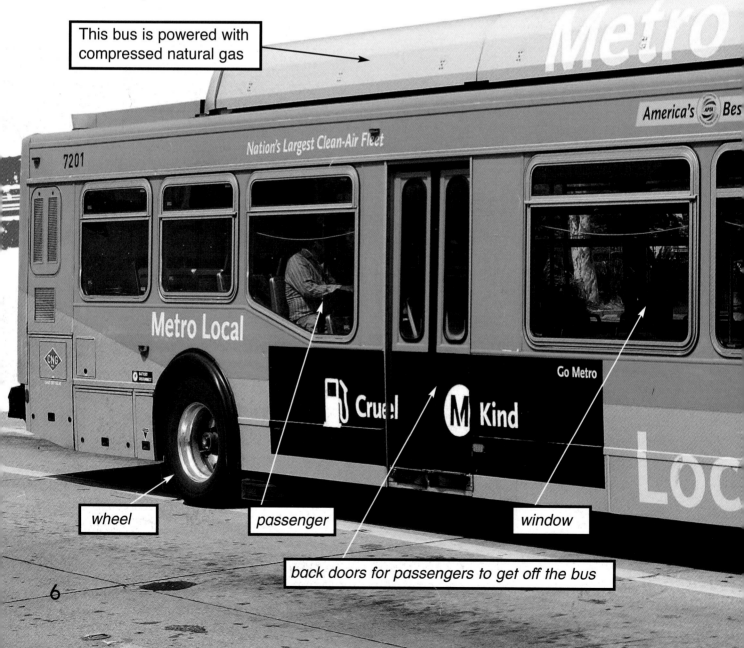

This bus is powered with compressed natural gas

wheel

passenger

window

back doors for passengers to get off the bus

People movers

People get on and off a bus through a door near the front of the bus. Some buses also have doors at the back for people to exit from. Inside there are seats for passengers to sit on. Some buses even have washrooms.

bus driver

destination sign

front doors for passengers to get on the bus

bike rack

Public transportation

Buses are one type of vehicle used for public transportation. Public transportation is a way to move many people from one place to another within a city. Public means that everyone can use it. People pay money to use public transportation.

Buses make traveling around a big city easier.

Good for everyone

Public transportation is good for the environment. When many people share one ride there are fewer vehicles on the road. This means fewer traffic jams and fewer parked cars. One bus also causes less pollution than many cars.

A bus runs on a schedule and makes set stops along a route.

Transit buses

Transit buses are used for public transportation. *Transit* means to move a person or thing. Transit buses make short trips within a city. Sometimes they are called city buses. They have low floors so people can get on and off easily.

A transit bus has doors at the front for people getting on and doors in the middle for people getting off.

The "fare" way to go

Passengers have to pay a fare to ride on a transit bus. There is a fare box at the front of the bus. Passengers put a ticket or money inside the box. Some passengers use a pass card to show they have paid.

fare box

Transit buses have bars and handles for people to hold onto when they have to stand.

handle

bar

Paratransit

Paratransit is public transport for people with special needs. Passengers with disabilities cannot always get on or off a transit bus easily. **Paratransit buses** have special equipment to make using public transit easier.

wheelchair accessible symbol

ramp

Buses equipped with wheelchair ramps make it easier for people who use wheelchairs to get on and off a bus.

Getting a lift

Smaller buses called minibuses are often used for paratransit. Most have wheelchair lifts or ramps for people who use wheelchairs. Sometimes, taxis or minivans are used for paratransit, too.

wheelchair lift

A wheelchair lift allows a wheelchair and the person sitting in it to be raised and lowered into and out of the bus or van.

Many public transportation systems also include paratransit vehicles.

Articulated buses

An **articulated bus** has two parts. Articulated means that it bends in the middle. The front of the bus has an engine. It pulls a trailer that is attached at a joint. The joint is where the bus bends. This helps the bus turn around city corners.

The joint is covered with a folded panel that bends, too.

joints

trailers

Bi-articulated buses pull two trailers behind them.

All folded up

Articulated buses carry more passengers than regular buses because they are longer. Sometimes, they are called caterpillar buses. These buses are used for public transportation.

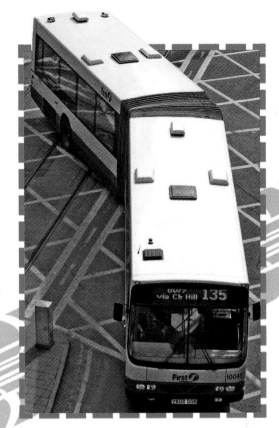

An articulated bus can carry up to 200 passengers.

Trolleybuses

Trolleybuses are powered by electricity. They have trolley poles that reach up from the roof to wires overhead. Trolleybuses get electricity from these wires. The electricity powers the motor. Having electric motors mean trolleybuses run very quietly.

Trolleybuses get electricity from nearby power plants.

Trolleybuses take in electricity from the wires overhead.

Trolley transit

Trolleybuses make short trips around the city. They are used for public transport. They do not pollute the air. Trolleybuses can travel up steep hills easier than other vehicles. Their rubber wheels grip the ground better when they travel uphill.

Trolleybuses are often used in cities with steep hills, such as San Francisco.

Electric streetcars

A **streetcar** is another kind of electric-powered vehicle used for public transportation. It is sometimes called a tram. Streetcars have steel wheels and ride on two steel tracks in streets. They get electric power from a trolley pole that reaches up to overhead wires.

Streetcars are used for public transportation in large cities.

Right on track

Streetcars can only move on tracks. They cannot pull over to the side of the road as buses do. Instead, people have to walk out onto the street to get on or off. Some streetcar stops have islands or platforms in the middle of the road for passengers to wait safely.

overhead wire

Streetcars are powered by electricity from overhead wires.

island

This streetcar stops at an island to let passengers get on and off.

Subway trains

Subways are another type of public transportation. Subway trains travel on two or three steel railway tracks. They move a lot of people over short distances very quickly. There are seats for people to sit on inside each railcar. Subway trains can carry a lot of people at one time. They are sometimes called people movers.

FINCH

Above and below

Sometimes subway trains travel in tunnels under a city. The also travel on bridges above a city. Subway railcars are joined together. Each one gets electric power from the tracks they ride on.

Passengers can stand while the train is moving by holding on to bars.

An elevated train above street level does not get in the way of cars or people crossing the street.

School buses

School buses take children to and from school. Most school buses are yellow. Yellow is an easy color to see at all times. School buses come in different sizes. Full-sized school buses hold from 40 to 48 students. Minibuses hold up to 15 students.

School buses are also used to take students on field trips.

stop sign

Safe and sound

All school buses have special equipment to help keep passengers safe. School buses have emergency exit doors at the back. They also have a stop arm with flashing lights that swings out. This tells drivers to stop their cars when passengers are getting on or off the school bus.

Passengers get on and off the bus through the side door at the front.

Coach buses

Coach buses carry passengers on longer trips. They usually travel between cities. Some buses travel to different countries. People buy tickets to the places they want to go. A round-trip ticket means the passenger rides to a place and then returns home on a later bus.

Passengers get on and off the same door on a coach bus.

Riding in comfort!

Coach buses have special features to make passengers more comfortable. Many have air conditioning and washrooms. Some have personal reading lights and video screens for watching movies. Coach buses often make long trips.

Passengers on this coach bus can watch movies on the large video screen.

Passengers keep large suitcases in storage areas underneath the floor of coach buses.

Touring buses

Touring buses travel between cities. Touring buses are privately owned or rented by a group of people for private use. Musical groups and sports teams often use touring buses to travel between locations.

inside a touring bus

A great way to go

People often live on touring buses as they travel. Some of these buses have kitchens, beds, and televisions. Groups of people sometimes rent touring buses for sightseeing.

Double-decker buses

Double-decker buses
are vehicles that have
two floors or decks on
top of one another. These
buses have stairs that lead
to the second floor. Most double-decker
buses have a roof over the top floor. Some
have an open roof so passengers can
enjoy a view of the city as they travel.

Double-decker buses are used in many countries all over the world.

Twice the fun

Double-decker buses make short trips around town. They are used for public transportation. Some coach buses are also double-deckers. Passengers on the top floor get the best view!

These passengers are entering the rear door of a double-decker bus.

These passengers are entering the front door of an open-roof double-decker sightseeing bus.

Cable cars

A **cable car** is a vehicle
that is pulled by a cable.
A cable is a very strong rope
made of metal. Cable cars ride on rails or
tracks in a road. The cable runs inside a
channel between the tracks in the road.

San Fransisco is the only city in North America to still have cable cars in service.

Cable cars can go up very steep hills.

Getting a grip

A cable car has no engine. The engine at a power house moves the cable. The power house is a building that has large wheels and engines that move the cable. The cable always moves at the same speed. The cable car grips the moving cable to go forward. It lets the cable go when it needs to stop.

Words to know and Index

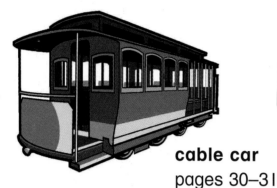

cable car
pages 30–31

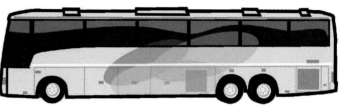

coach bus
pages 24–25

double-decker bus
pages 28–29

paratransit bus
pages 12–13

streetcar
pages 18–19

transit bus
pages 10, 11, 17